Amazon FBA

A Retail Arbitrage Blueprint

A Guide to the Secret Business of Retail Arbitrage and Selling on Amazon

By

Scott Daily

Disclaimer

I dedicate this book to my children. They are the sole reason for my existence.

Contents

INTRODUCTION

Today's world is very different from that of yesteryears. Normally when a line like that is written, it is promptly followed with some sort of devastating description of the "good ole days" and how things were so much better back then as compared to now. However, that is just not the case at this point in time. Actually, today is far better in terms of resources and opportunities than it has been in the last one hundred years. At least, that is, when it comes to the subject of personal income and wealth.

We all remember the 90's right? We watched mom and dad go to work every day from 8 or 9 in the morning until 4 or 5 at night. Then they would come home and go about the rest of their evening. Every week it was the same dollar amount being deposited into their checking account, and from that amount they lived and supported their families. Now, that way of life is still very much the way many people choose to structure their income and wealth today, and that is quite fine. However, for those of us that want something different, that want something more, that want to create our own wealth, or create our own business, we have options. Going back to the 90's again, if at that time you wanted to have some more income or increase your wealth you essentially had only one option: go out and get a second job. Today, that second job for a lot of people is spending a couple hours every night sitting in front of their computer after their kids go to bed. I am one of those people. I have a fantastic career in sales with a fantastic company. I work every day from 7:30 am to 5:00 pm and I am very comfortable with the amount of money I make in a given year. In addition to this, I have something completely different that I do as well. I am an internet entrepreneur, and through this book, I intend to show you how I do it, and hopefully provide you with some information that can help you along in your journey of what I like to call "making your second living."

PART ONE

A Guide to the Secret Business of Retail Arbitrage

CHAPTER ONE

What is Retail Arbitrage?

Retail Arbitrage, or RA as it is commonly referred to, is the art and science of finding items locally on retail store shelves that you can flip and sell for a profit online by way of Amazon and eBay. You just read the absolute most important line in this entire book. That is right - the very first line of chapter one also happens to be the most important. Hence, I will repeat it; Retail Arbitrage is the art and science of finding items locally on retail store shelves that you can flip and sell for a profit online by way of Amazon and eBay.

By definition arbitrage means the simultaneous buying and selling of securities, currency, or commodities in different markets or in derivative forms in order to take advantage of differing prices for the same asset. Admittedly, that definition is a bit daunting. Therefore, allow me to rephrase it more appropriately for the purpose of this book. Retail arbitrage is when you buy items that are on sale for less at your local store than they're selling for online, and then resell them on the internet for a profit. Your partner in this venture just happens to be the the world's largest online retailer, Amazon.com.

It's never been necessarily easy to do RA, but it's a simple concept to understand. This is perhaps why some people have been taking advantage of it for a couple of decades. It's also been a viable sourcing option for that same length of time. Along with many other experts in the online selling industry, I believe that RA will always be an opportunity as long as there are relatively free markets in operation.

What would you do if you saw money simply laying in the aisle of your local mall or big-box retailer? I'm not talking about a few coins or dollars either. I'm talking fives, tens, twenties, fifties, even one hundred dollar bills. Would you take the time to bend down and pick them up, or would you just continue shopping? It's a ridiculous question, isn't it?

In order to better comprehend this principle as it relates to the retail world, let's take a real-life example of mine:

> I like to shop the big box stores in my town. I will not say exactly which store I was in because these stores do not like to have their names mentioned when it comes to retail arbitrage. But for the sake of painting the picture adequately and as full as possible, let's just say this store is definitely one you have heard of and likely have shopped in as it is one of the biggest retail stores in the world. I walked in on a Friday night and did my usual routine of checking all the aisles that they typically shelve their clearance items on and came across ten men's beard shavers that normally sell for $129.99. Luckily, this store was clearancing them out for $35.00. Now, some quick math tells us that there is roughly $95.00 between what this store was selling these shavers at and the retail price. The question I had to answer while I was in the store was, how much are these shavers selling for online? I pulled out my cell phone and scanned the barcode into my Amazon Sellers App, and instantly saw that they were selling for around $99.00 on Amazon.com. I loaded my cart with all ten. After it was all said and done I spent about $350.00 on the shavers. It cost $5.00 to ship them to Amazon FBA (more on FBA later), and about $200.00 in Amazon selling fees. My total out-of-pocket costs, $555.00. I brought in about $990.00 in sales. Subtract the cost from the sales and you have a profit of about $430.00. The total amount of time I spent purchasing, packing and shipping the items was roughly 45 minutes. Hence, for this transaction my hourly rate of pay was $573.33. That is roughly what big-time Wall Street Attorneys make on an hourly basis. I'll take it!

In some stores, you will be able to see these items priced way below the manufacturer's suggested retail price aka MSRP. Technically, if you have funds to invest, you can just buy these items and sell them to other buyers at or a little below the MSRP as I did in the above example. As you likely notice, the whole process is highly concentrated on the ability to flip the item, but as soon as you have a viable product, you are more or less assured of a decent profit.

CHAPTER TWO

How Sustainable is the Business of RA?

I'll make my case for the long-term stability of RA below as briefly as I can. If you grasp the basics of free trade economics it will really help this chapter to soak in. If the basics of economics are foreign concepts to you, it might not make as much sense, but we aren't talking rocket science here either.

First, a bit of history of the retail arbitrage opportunity:

RA first popped up online as a viable way to earn a nice living nearly a couple of decades ago. Since that time on Amazon, eBay, and many other online selling platforms, we've seen billions of dollars of product move from retail stores to enterprising entrepreneurs like us, then on to Amazon or eBay, and then of course finally to consumers.

From where I sit, the only way RA will ever die is if free markets die, and I do not know about you, but I for one will need to be dragged kicking and screaming at every step if this occurs.

The "supposed" threats against RA are as follows:

Competition: This theory says that so many of us are doing RA that the opportunity will soon die or become unviable. The same argument has been around for about 15 years. Based on my own experience, there is enough retail markdown opportunity to support a lot of RA entrepreneurs. Plus, think of it like this - if retail stores keep clearance pricing items for quick sale, the price on Amazon will go lower and lower. This will cause more and more consumers to move from the retail marketplace to Amazon. Hence, causing even more clearance and markdown opportunities in the retail market. Don't think this could happen based on a few people searching for deals? Ask yourself this: how did Amazon become the largest e-retailer in the world? It wasn't by charging the same price that people pay at their local brick-and-mortar store.

Brand Protection: Brands are being protective of their goods & price points and some are now going direct to Amazon, which they hope will make it harder for us as RA sellers to find and sell profitable brands online. In other words, they are trying to cut out the middle man. That happens to be us.

The "new" vs. "used" goods debate: This is a continuation of the brand protection argument. Brands want to force us as sellers (often in cooperation with Amazon) to call otherwise brand-new RA products something less than "brand new" once we pull them off the shelves. From their point of view, the argument is that an item can only be sold as "new" once. Therefore, when we buy it, it is no longer new. Now, while I do not agree with this definition of new, I do see the argument they are presenting. Additionally, I think that over the next several years, Amazon will lend itself to that definition as well. However, when Amazon does this it will have huge effects on their sales because it will drive consumers back to the brick-and-mortar retailers. Therefore, I ascertain that in the event the definition of "new" is refined by Amazon, they will in turn be forced to offer an additional selling condition called something like "New Other." It is in this condition where RA sellers will have to sell their products. Believe me when I tell you, it will not take long at all for the Amazon consumers to understand that the difference between "new" and "new other" is non-existent, and in turn, RA will continue to live on and prosper!

When it comes to retail arbitrage, the name of the game is to buy low, sell high. You are not buying the season's bestsellers off the shelf to resell; instead, you are shopping the best sales and bartering for the best deals. That's what makes this such a popular side hustle for the bargain hunters, single parents, stay-at-home parents and more. A lot of us are the primary shoppers in our households. We know how to not only save a buck, but we can probably save several! So the question becomes, if we can do that, why not reverse the process and use that skill to begin making a really solid income?

CHAPTER THREE

Where to Buy Low-Priced Items to Sell

1. Going out of business sales - Big stuff can be sold locally on Craigslist or Facebook Groups, other stuff can go to Amazon.

2. Clearance Racks – This is your bread and butter as an RA entrepreneur. The items on clearance racks are usually new and in great condition with barcodes. I focus most of my attention on clearance items.

3. Garage Sales – Be the early bird.

4. Thrift Stores - Go often, as new items are put on the shelves every day. Understand that you may lose some money on some items, but the profit margin on other items will be so huge that it won't even matter. I once bought a print cartridge for $5.00 and sold it the same day on eBay for $120.00.

5. Auctions – While this is a decent option and I know some people that do very well with auctions as a way to source products, I have found them to be too time consuming.

6. Flea markets

7. Dropshipping – Identify online sources for clearance items, and sell them as a seller fulfilled item on Amazon. When the order comes in, just cut and paste the address information from Amazon to the site, and make a record of the tracking number to upload. You never touch the item, you just collect the profit.

8. Wholesale Companies

9. Discount bookstores – The book market is huge. Remember, this is how Amazon started!

10. Scanner Monkey - You are not going to want to tell anyone else about this site.

11. Classified Ads

12. Estate Sales

13. Libraries - They often give books away for micro-amounts of money, or sometimes they give them away free. You can make a bundle here in volume alone. You can sell the book on Amazon for $0.01 and make $2 to $3 just on the shipping credit.

14. Outlet Malls – Fantastic source. Be sure to look for mall-wide seasonal sales.

15. Big Box Retailers - This is where I clean up on the clearance items.

16. Buy on Amazon to sell on eBay and vice versa - Simple, find items you can make a couple bucks on, then list them on the opposite site. When your item sells, purchase the item and change the ship to address to the purchaser's address that bought it from you. This is arbitrage trading at its best. I spent the first 3 years of my RA business doing this exactly. I made a killing!

17. Liquidation Stores - Great places but be careful, as they often have expired goods. You can't sell expired merchandise.

18. Costco and Sam's Club – You can just about operate your entire RA business out of these stores. Take some time to walk around and do some scanning. You will be shocked at how much profit is simply laying around.

19. Black Friday sales!

CHAPTER FOUR

Requirements For Deciding What To Buy And Sell

I am going to break down each product requirement and explain the reasoning behind each one, as then it will be easy to see what product requirements are vital to have. I must make it clear though, these are just the requirements I have identified. You can tweak these or come up with your own. It all depends on what you are trying to accompolish with your RA business.

Requirements That are Very Important for Success

The requirements that are going to be listed below are considered to be very important for success and I would highly suggest that the product you are going to sell meets most, if not all of the requirements below.

1. Average Product Sale Price Between $15-$500

The selling price for your product is a very important thing to know and it is something you must know before you make a purchase. The $15-$500 price range is the sweet spot for pricing because in today's high-tech world people are willing to spend this amount of money online. The reason the minimum threshold is $15 is because any lower than that will yield too little profit. When you are making an RA purchase you basically need to buy the product at around 33% of the selling price or less. When you do this you will pay roughly 33% to Amazon in selling fees, 33% to recoup the investment in purchasing the product, and 33% goes into your pocket as profit. Hence, if the item you are purchasing is selling for $15, that means you must buy this product for $5 at most. In this generic transaction you would pay $5 to Amazon, $5 back to your business for the investment of buying the inventory aka the product, and there would be $5 left over in profit. That is why I feel $15 is the minimum price threshold, because based on those numbers it yields a nice $5 profit.

As for the maximum threshold of $500, I use this amount because it is as much as I am willing to risk. For me personally I do not like to risk much more than $300 to $400 on any one single item, as when I do, I feel I am too susceptible to taking a loss on product returns or malfunctions. Amazon has a 60-day return policy, and when items get returned, unless Amazon identifies that they are the cause of the return, you must incur that cost. Don't let that scare you. Returns are minimal. Now, to the astute reader you may have noticed that I mentioned earlier that you must buy a product at 33% or lower than the selling price. One thing to remember is that as the selling price on Amazon goes up, so does the percentage at which you can invest and still make a good profit. Consider the following example:

> I purchased again from a major retailer 4 cameras over the course of several weeks. Each of these cameras were selling for $339 on Amazon. I purchased them from the retailer on clearance at a price of roughly $199. That is about 59% of the selling value. After selling the item at around $339 I paid about $28 in Amazon fees, and $199 to recover the cost of each camera. Hence, I had $102 in profit leftover for each camera sold. Ultimately I invested $796 to earn $408 in profit. The total process took around one week to do, and during that week I I spent about 1 hour on these 4 transactions combined. Ha! How many Wall Street stockbrokers are pulling in those kind of returns? Bernie Madoff excluded that is.

The reason this percentage of the selling price can be so high is that Amazon does not stick to a 33% fees rate for all their items. As the selling price goes up the fee rate % goes way down. As you can see, for this item their fee rate was less than 10%. I love Amazon!

2. Lightweight and Relatively Small

Ideally you want your product to be as light as possible. I would say that anything over 10 to 15 pounds is too heavy unless you are planning on selling the product for a higher price. Similarly, you do not want the product to be too big either. The more a product weighs, the more it is going to cost you to ship either to your customer or to Amazon FBA. The bigger your product is, the more it is going to cost you to ship.

> I once purchased 15 different infant play mats that came in boxes that were roughly 36 in x 36 in x 4 in. The selling price of these items was well above my 33% rule so I jumped on the chance to buy them, as each one only weighed about 3 pounds. That is the last time I make that mistake! Since the items were so big, shipping them to Amazon cost me around 3 times what I actually paid for the products. After all was said and done, I ended up losing about $12 on each of these items for a total loss of around $170.

Take it from me, there are some risks involved in RA. You can avoid them by paying attention and learning from other people's mistakes.

3. Products Have a 50,000 Best Seller Rank or Lower in their Main Category

It is very hard to get a good estimate of how well a certain product is selling on Amazon, but the best thing Amazon gives is the best seller rank (BSR). The BSR lets you see how well that individual product is selling within its category. For example, a product with a BSR of 20,000 is going to sell a lot less than a product in the same category with a BSR of 2,000.

This is useful for us as sellers because we can determine whether there is demand for this product in the market or not. That is why it is vital to go after a product that has demand in the market. And that is where the BSR comes in - it gives us a good look at whether there is demand for the product or not.

From my research, people say many different things when it comes to the minimum BSR of a product for it to be viable to sell. Some say below 10,000 BSR while others say 500-2,000 BSR. I also saw people saying that a product with a 50,000 BSR and below is good and that is what I am going to suggest as well since it is the number I tend to use as I make my decisions.

Again, I want to reiterate that this is not a hard and fast rule. I routinely buy products that are 100,000 plus on the BSR rank. However, when I do this I do so knowing that I may have to sit on the product for a while. Since this is the case, I want a fair amount of upside potential in my profit. The reverse is also true. If I buy an item that is in the top ten of the Amazon BSR rank, I am willing to sacrifice my profit margin greatly if necessary. The reason? I know it will sell instantaneously. I will push small margins for fast movement, and take large margins for slow movement.

Ideally, when you search for your product keyword in Amazon the first couple of results (2-3) will all have BSRs lower than 50,000 for the main category. The more products below 50,000, the better. This proves that there are a ton of people buying these products, which means that if you can get into the same position as these products then you will be able to sell a ton as well.

4. The Product can be Purchased for 33% or Less of Sale Price

This is a way to quickly estimate that the profit margins will be good on a potential product. I have explained this in several examples throughout this book. Trust me, when you start to go out and search for your RA deals, you will see how important this is. Additionally, it will become second nature to you very quickly.

5. Year-Round Seller (Not Seasonal)

It is not vital, but I prefer to sell products that sell year round compared to seasonally. Personally, I would rather go after selling a product that I know will sell fairly consistently all throughout the year so that I can make money anytime.

6. Similar Products Being Sold on eBay

If similar products to the product you are considering are being sold on eBay then you can assume that the market for your product is big. It is a good sign that there is demand for your product if people are selling similar products on platforms other than Amazon. This isn't a major requirement to determine the success of your product, but like I said, it is a good sign to see similar products being sold on eBay. A quick way to check is to head over to eBay and type in your product keyword. If you see sellers then you are good to go.

Another nice thing to consider is that in the event you take a return from Amazon on a product, you can turn around and list it as an auction on eBay. That way you will not take a complete loss on it. Currently I am in the habit of listing all of my returned items on eBay and I find that I recoup roughly 75% of the original purchase price by doing this. This can equate to thousands of dollars per year.

PART TWO

A Guide to Fulfillment By Amazon

aka FBA

CHAPTER FIVE

Drop Shipping: The Amazon FBA Way

The Amazon FBA program stands for Fulfillment by Amazon. This is a service Amazon provides to allow online and offline sellers to send their goods to Amazon, and Amazon will pack and ship the products to individual customers on your behalf. You may not yet be aware of how big the Amazon marketplace is if you don't visit there regularly. They have come a long way from just selling books, to now selling just about anything.

You can also sell products on Amazon and not use their FBA service, so you ship your own products, but there are many advantages of using the FBA system, which will free up your time and provide greater opportunity to be either out looking for more RA products, or just enjoying the free time that FBA creates.

It is really a similar service that other drop shippers provide, but Amazon holds your goods in one of their fulfillment centers. The service will send your goods anytime and to anywhere on your behalf. The costs for the service are very competitive, and you only pay for actual storage and shipments at discounted Amazon rates. They do not charge a fee to use the system.

Why It Works With Amazon FBA Drop Shipping

The principles of buy low/sell high are very much in effect online! You can easily join the rush to make money online by applying the very simple principles of buy low/sell high! Fulfillment By Amazon has made making a nice profit on ordinary items that you purchase locally a real possibility.

Retail arbitrage is not a new idea, but it has taken on a new meaning using the internet as your marketplace. You can easily buy items locally at deep discounts from various avenues, as discussed in part one, and then resell them for a profit using Amazon FBA.

CHAPTER SIX

What Will You Need Before you Start FBA?

As you start your FBA business there are certain supplies that you are inevitably going to need. Listed below are the tools I find most useful. All of these tools can be purchased by going to www.workbungalow.com/store. Here you will be able to see these products first hand and purchase them through Amazon easily.

1. **Postal Scale** - You will need a postal scale that can weigh packages that are at least fifty pounds. Fifty pounds is the most that a package can weigh when shipping it to FBA if the package consists of more than one type of item. In the event the package is full of the same item, it can weigh more than fifty pounds but must be marked with the words "TEAM LIFT." While fifty pounds is the minimum weight a scale should be able to accommodate, I recommend going higher than that. The scale I use can weigh packages up to 125 pounds. I like this because I do from time to time send packages that are over 50 pounds in weight.

2. **Scotty Peelers** - These are tools used for peeling stickers and price tags off of packages. You will quickly find that Scotty Peelers are going to be one of your most valuable tools when it comes to retail arbitrage, as FBA will not allow any prices or tags on their products.

3. **Goo Gone** - This is used in combination with Scotty Peelers and is used to remove sticky residue left behind from stickers or tags on your items. Amazon will not allow residue on their items.

4. **Laser Printer or Dymo 450 Thermal Printer** - This one is debatable. Many FBA sellers use these printers because of the labels they must print off and put on each product that is shipped to Amazon. I actually opt to have Amazon label my products for me. They will do this for the small fee of $0.20 per item. At first I thought this was expensive, but since I have started letting Amazon take care of this for me it has saved me hours upon hours each month. The reason your labels must be printed on a laser or thermal printer is because the writing will not smear with them. If you use an inkjet printer, smearing becomes a risk. If you already own an inkjet printer and would like to do this, you can do so by covering each label with clear tape prior to attaching to the actual product, as this will stop any smearing that may occur with the ink.

5. **Avery 5160 Shipping Labels** - These again you may not need if you decide to have Amazon do your labeling for you. If you opt to do it yourself, these are the size labels you will need.

6. **Excel Accounting Sheets** - These can be downloaded for free at our website www.workbungalow.com using the coupon code 7DAYS. These will be used for keeping your finances straight. You will need to know if you are making money on a monthly basis and you will also need everything organized when tax season comes around. Hence, having organized, easy-to-use spreadsheets are a must.

7. **Filing Box or Folders** - Similar to the Excel spreadsheets, this is for keeping everything organized. As you get into the business of retail arbitrage you will accumulate an extremely large number of receipts. You will need to save all receipts as proof of purchase to keep on file to accompany your taxes in case you are ever audited. In addition to this you may want to keep hard copies of tracking receipts and emails if applicable.

8. **Packing Material** - This is really based on how you like to pack things. I always have on hand an assortment of boxes, as well as packing tape, Scotch tape, a tape gun, copy paper, assorted poly bags, and bubble wrap. You can really blow your budget here, so search for bargains. You can check our shipping center at www.workbungalow.com for links to various well-priced shipping material.

9. **Computer** - This is something you likely already have. Make sure it is in good working order. A slow computer will make your retail arbitrage business take too long, and that is the exact opposite of what you want. Quick is good, slow is dead!

10. **Payment Method** - You will need a credit card or debit card for all of the online purchases you will be making. Additionally, using this instead of cash is a good way to keep everything organized.

11. **Bank Account** - I recommend maintaining a separate bank account for Amazon to deposit and withdraw funds.

CHAPTER SEVEN

Setting Up Your Basic Amazon Seller's Account

he first step to setting up your Retail Arbitrage business is getting rganized and ready to start selling on Amazon. We are going to spend this hapter discussing exactly how to do that. The ultimate goal for this usiness is to make money while working as few hours as possible. I like to ork on my retail arbitrage business for no more than ten hours per week. Jith that in mind, let's start looking at getting organized in a manner that ill allow us to build toward that goal of 2 hours per night (or 10 hours per eek assuming you are working 5 nights each week).

he first thing you need is a suitable work area. For me it is my bedroom. or you, it may be a dining room, study, or basement. Anywhere is fine, ut the main attribute needed is that there is room for you to spread out. ou will need access to your computer, printer, and other tools, so an area ith a closet or a set of shelves will also be helpful. In addition to ample omputer space you will need an area in which you can pack relatively large oxes. We will discuss the details of packing boxes later, but for now, trust ne when I say that you will need some space. I use the floor in my bedroom or this area. You will also need a place to store your miscellaneous upplies. I use a computer desk with drawers for this. Anything will work. have seen people use file boxes and tool boxes for the same purpose. astly, you will need an area in which to store your inventory. By the time ou get through chapter 8, you should be using FBA for 90% of your sales. lence, keeping a large inventory on hand is not something you will need to o, and it certainly is not something you want to do. However, you will have ome leftover products, or products that you are selling on other platforms that will need to be stored. For this, I use a 4' x 4' corner of my bedroom. I know, pretty fancy right?

After all is said and done I can sum up your spacial needs in one sentence. You need a work area in which you can have a computer and printer, a small space to store products, and a small space to pack boxes.

Once you have identified the area in which you are going to work, you are now ready to organize the administrative aspects of your business.

Organizing Your Financial Records

One very important part of an at-home e-commerce business is that you keep meticulous records. First of all you will need these to figure out whether you are profitable or not. Second, you will need all this info when tax season comes around. In my opinion the practice of keeping thorough records is what separates a successful retail arbitrage business from a failing one. There is no quicker way to kill your e-commerce endeavor than by losing money and not knowing it.

In order to keep these records you are going to need some basic accounting spreadsheets. All of these can be downloaded for free at www.workbungalow.com using the promo code 7DAYS at checkout. You will need the following:
1. Cost of Goods Sold or COGS
2. Inventory Record
3. Expense and Income Ledger aka General Ledger
4. Profit and Loss Statement

In addition to these spreadsheets you will need a good way to keep all receipts as these will need to be available in case of an IRS audit of your business. Therefore, you will need a folder, box, envelope, etc. that will be easily accessible to store any and all receipts for expenses.

Setting Up Your Amazon Seller's Account

I could spend the next four to five pages going step by step on how to set up an Amazon Seller's Account. However, I am not going to do that. The fact of the matter is that today's world does not lend itself to hand holding when it comes to web-based systems. Most of you likely already know that it is easier to get on and just figure it out then it is to read a step-by-step guide. If you happen to be one of the few that would prefer a step-by-step guide on this process, let me break the news to you: that is just not how it is done anymore. Step-by-step guides might as well be delivered on the back of a dinosaur. Diving into an e-commerce business is going to require a lot of getting to know your programs on your own. Hence, let's start here. I will say this: if you do get hung up on this process Amazon is very good with customer service. Go to the 'contact us' tab and opt to have them call you. You will enter your number and they will reach out to you within seconds.

As you get into this process you will notice that Amazon is asking whether you want a personal or professional account. The professional account costs $39.99 per month as of the publishing date of this book. Getting the professional account and paying the monthly fee is an absolute must! You will recoup the $39.99 monthly fee in no time, as products sell at lightning speeds on Amazon. Additionally, you are not eligible for FBA without a professional account.

When you elect to go with the professional account you will be asked for your business name and tax identification number. There is a good chance that you do not currently have either of these. Choose a catchy business name and instead of a tax identification number you can use your social security number. Eventually, you will want to incorporate your business once you have gotten used to retail arbitrage and FBA, and decided it is a worthwhile endeavor. I personally formed an LLC in 2012 so that I could keep things nice and neat for my taxes. Additionally, I wanted a certain level of separation between my personal wealth and my business liabilities. I used an attorney and this cost me around $1000. You can do the same thing for around $200 plus any state fees on legal websites such as legalzoom.com if you do not want to go with an attorney.

Listing Your First Item

Once you have worked through the set-up process on Amazon it is time to list your first product. I know, you may not have been expecting that, but hey, there is no time like the present! What is holding you back? Get up right now and go find something in your house that is new and unopened that you do not want. It is time for you to list it. Again, I am not going to walk you through how to do this step by step. I will give you a couple of quick pointers though:

1. Start from your Seller Dashboard and go to the upper-left-hand corner of the page to the drop-down menu titled *Inventory*.
2. Select *Add a product*.
3. Follow the rest of the prompts paying particular attention to the required fields denoted in red highlights on the product information screen.

Congratulations! What you just did was list an item in the traditional *Seller Fulfilled* manner. Once your item sells, you will receive an email notification that you need to ship that item.

Shipping Your First Item

From your seller dashboard again:
1. Drop down the menu item titled *Orders*.
2. Select *Manage Orders*.
3. Select the order you wish to ship.
4. Follow prompts from there.

I always recommend buying shipping through Amazon as to the best of my knowledge it is the cheapest way to go.

Once you have shipped your first item the payment will appear in your Amazon account. You will see that Amazon automatically takes out any fees they are owed and the rest goes to you. Based on my experience it is easy to see your account balance grow to $6000 to $7000 dollars each month. Not bad for ten hours of work a week!

You could basically operate your Amazon RA business in exactly that manner and do very, very well with it. Having said that, there is a much easier and more profitable way to structure your business. You guessed it. FBA baby!

I waited three years before dabbling in FBA. Within a week I was kicking myself for waiting so long. As previously mentioned FBA is the same as selling with the Seller Fulfilled method of Amazon, except you do not handle the shipment, returns, or customer service of any of your items. Amazon does it all for you!

CHAPTER EIGHT

Setting Up Your FBA Account

Once you have gone through the process of setting up and completing your first sale as an Amazon seller via the Seller Fulfilled method, it is time to start setting up your FBA account. FBA is similar to Seller Fulfilled sales in that you still source products the same way that was laid out in part one of this book. Additionally, you still use Amazon as your primary selling platform. The key difference between the Seller Fulfilled method and the FBA method is the manner in which you handle the products and transactions.

As you will recall from the previous chapter, as a Seller Fulfilled seller you basically handle everything to do with the entire transaction. You source the product, list it, inventory it, pack it, buy postage, ship it, upload tracking information, monitor tracking information, and handle all returns and customer inquiries. FBA greatly reduces this process. As an FBA seller you will source the product, list the product, and make a bulk shipment of many various products to Amazon fulfillment centers. Then you're done.

Again, similar to the previous chapters I am not going to waste time walking you through how to set up your account so that you can take advantage of FBA. Rather, I am going to rely on you to be able to sort that through. What I will do is walk you through a few key points of the process of setting up your shipments, and give you some pointers on how I do things so as to keep your time usage as low as possible.

As you start to go through the process of becoming FBA approved I recommend that you select certain settings. To adjust these settings you will need to go to the upper-right-hand corner of your Amazon Seller's Dashboard and hover over "settings", then select "Fulfillment By Amazon." From there you will see a series of settings that you can manipulate.

Under the "Optional Settings" I recommend enabling "MWS Label Service", as well as choosing Merchant for "Who Preps" and "Who Labels." Now I rarely prep or label any of my shipments, but I still recommend this as being the default setting and manually changing it as you create shipments. I like to do it this way because it forces me to think for each shipment of whether I am truly willing to spend the money on these services, as they are not free. On a side note, I always choose to have Amazon prep and label because their prices are so inexpensive, and it saves me hours upon hours of work.

Under "Inbound Settings" I leave the "Inventory Placement Option" on its default setting and make sure that "Show Restricted Item Warnings" and "Show Listing Approval Warnings" are enabled. This keeps it so that you will not inadvertently try to sell an item for which you are not approved.

Under the "Repackaging Settings" I make sure that "Repackage Unsellable Customer Returns" and "Auto Enrol in Newly Added Categories" are enabled. I pretty much disable everything else with one MAJOR exception. That is I make sure to enable "Amazon Partnered LTL Service. This is the setting that allows you to take advantage of the extremely deep discounts Amazon offers to its FBA sellers when shipping to an Amazon fulfillment center. Additionally, I would like to call special attention to the "Commingled Inventory" option. Make sure this is disabled. My opinion is that commingled inventory is for people that do not maintain proper integrity of their products. If you choose to sell in commingled inventory you will risk being held accountable for someone else's poor judgement on item condition.

CHAPTER NINE

Shipping Your First FBA Shipment

Now that we have set up our FBA account and selected certain important settings I am going to walk you through the process of creating a shipment. This I feel is the part of Amazon FBA that can be a little daunting, and as such, I think some general step-by-step instruction can help you to avoid some of the time-consuming pitfalls into which I fell. I will structure this process as a numeric step-by-step generic guidline. Here we go:

1. **Source your products** – Refer to part one of this book. A key point here is that with Amazon FBA you do not need to sell all of the same product. When I go out on my retail arbitrage hunts I will buy ten, twenty and sometimes even more different types of products. They may be baby items, tools, cookware, toys, etc. They all get packed and shipped together. So for step one, the sky is the limit.

2. **Prepare your purchased items** – You must make sure that there are not price tags or merchant-specific stickers of any kind on your products. By merchant-specific stickers I mean anything that a big box retailers or individual store would put on the item. Barcodes and manufacturer stickers and/or tags should be left on. Everything else should be removed. Additionally, you must make sure that there is no sticker residue left behind on the product. I use Goo Gone to get residue off and it works great. If you fail to perform these two steps appropriately your items will be sent back to you and you will be charged for the return shipping. When I am doing this I find it is easiest to do all of the sticker and residue removal for all of the

products I am creating a shipment for at once. That way I can be most efficient.

3. **Add your products** – This is very similar to the way you added a product in the seller fulfilled chapter with a few extra steps.

    a. From your Amazon Seller Dashboard go to "Inventory".

    b. Select "Add a product".

    c. Type in your UPC code or description and identify your item and select "Sell yours". This will redirect you to the "Add offer info" page.

    d. From the "Add offer info page" the very first thing you need to do is scroll down to the section titled "Fulfillment Channel" and select "I want Amazon to ship and provide customer service for my items if they sell".

    e. Then select the appropriate condition of your item.

    f. Then set the price at which you want to sell your item. I recommend you click on "View Amazon Detail Page" at the top of the screen and setting your price to that of the lowest FBA Amazon Prime price. This should allow for maximum profit and limit the amount of pricing wars between you and other sellers.

    g. Scroll to the bottom of the page and select "Save and Finish". This will bring you to the FBA Inbound Workflow page.

    h. If this is your first product of the shipment select "create new shipment" If this is not the first product of a shipment you should be choosing "add to existing shipment".

    i. For packaging type you will likely need to choose "individual products". If you happen to be shipping many of the same product you can select "case pack". If you do this you must ship between 24 and 150 pieces to Amazon and you can not add any other prodcuts. Hence, these shipments will stand alone.

    j. Click "continue".

    k. Enter the quantity you are shipping.

    l. STOP! – Do not do anything else with this shipment at this point. Rather, repeat step 3 in its entirety for all of the products you are shipping in this shipment. Once you have completed adding all your products, click "continue" at the bottom of your product list, and move on to step 4.

4. **Prep your products** – At this step Amazon will offer some guidance on what prep work may need to be done to the products. My experience is that this is a rare occurrence, because I mostly sell new items. However, you basically have two options: you can do the prep work per Amazon's guidlines, or you can pay them to do it for you. I always choose the latter.

5. **Label your products** – At this step either you can label the products or Amazon can do it for $0.20 per item. My recommendation is to always pay Amazon to do this. It is money well spent both in time, and in the cost of labels and ink.

6. **Approve your shipment**

7. **Packing your shipment** – Once you have approved your shipment or shipments, you will need to go back in and select "work on shipment" for each shipment that has been created. To do this you:

   a. Pack the box with items as neatly and organized as possible, making sure to fill any leftover space in the box with paper, packing peanuts, or the like to help protect the items.

   b. Make sure the shipping service is set to "Amazon Partnered Carrier".

   c. Select "Everything in one box".

   d. Enter the package weight and dimensions and click "Confirm".

   e. Click "Calculate Payment".

   f. Approve charges.

   g. Print and adhere both box labels that print on the page.

   h. Click "Complete shipment".

   i. Click "Mark as shipped".

8. **Drop off at any UPS drop off site** - Make sure to get your receipt as proof that UPS did get your item from you!

9. **Sit back and watch the profits roll in!**

CHAPTER TEN

Helpful Tips

Below is a list of tips that I think are very useful when it comes to this whole process.

Expect to lose some money, especially at first.

This whole thing is a bit of a learning process for most of us. I know it certainly was for me. I still to this day will buy an item that is not selling as well as I thought, and I eventually have to take a little bit of a loss on it. Here is an example. Let's say you spend $50.00 on an item that you expect to sell for $100.00. You come to find out the item is listed at 100,000 in the kitchen appliance category rather than the home category like you thought. Now you will likely have to sit on it for a very long time, or you can discount it for quick sale. Either way, you are not going to lose your entire investment of $50.00. Let's say you discount it and it sells for $40.00. Ok, you lost $10.00. So ultimately you risked $10.00 to buy a $50.00 item that you were trying to sell for $100.00. I like that math!

Do not take returns personally.

Amazon is the biggest and best online retailer for many reasons. One of those reasons is that it is second to none in customer satisfaction. YOU ARE NOT THE CUSTOMER. Do not forget that! You are the supplier. The customer is the person buying your products from Amazon. They will return items from time to time. It is nothing personal, and the occurances of this are in my experience very infrequent.

Get the Amazon Seller app on your phone.

This is a must. I simply cannot go arbitrage hunting without it. This is the main tool for finding profit laying on the shelves as you hunt. Going without this would be like searching for jewlery on a beach without a metal detector.

Research on YouTube.

One of the best tools we have at our finger tips is YouTube. Get on and type in the search "Amazon FBA" and dozens of videos on how to do different things will come up. I personally recommend looking up Cody Hawk. This guy is the best resource I have found on the internet for learning the FBA process.

Don't be scared, but don't advertise what you are doing in the stores.

Don't get me wrong; the big box retailers know what you are doing when you are scanning items. As long as you are quiet and do not do something like video record yourself doing it to show your friends I doubt they will have a problem with it. Now, it is not illegal to participate in retail arbitrage, but that does not mean that the stores necessarily like it either. So be polite and courteous to everyone in the store, especially those employees that are helpful to you.

Get a Resale License

Right now you can buy products tax free if you are going to resell them if you have the appropriate license. If you do not have this you will lose 6 to 10 percent off your bottom line when buying retail items. You definitely can eat this percentage and still be profitable, but at $3000+ in purchases each month, 7% is a huge number!

Keep good records

Invest in a small business accounting textbook so that you can learn the basics of bookwork and accounting. This will allow you to know your business inside and out, and be extremely useful at tax time.

Seek other sources

There are hundreeds of books, videos and websites out there on the subject of RA, and FBA. Become a PHD on the subject by reading and studying everything you can. Every time I purchase a book or watch a video I find at least one helpful item in it. That over the course of the life of my business will yield thousands upon thousands of dollars in income.

Conclusion

The RA business is just the tip of the iceberg when it comes to generating income by way of the internet. We have all had thoughts before of how nice it would have been to get in early on certain endeavors. I often imagine what it would have been like to be ahead of the game when it comes to the dot com or the real estate booms in the nineties. Looking back on these times in history it is obvious that these extreme highs were followed by extreme lows and with good reason. What if though, you were the Mark Cuban of this era? Wise enough to witness a chance before it occurred, or in Mark's case a disaster before it unfolded. This is our chance! We are the profesionals that are here to witness the information age as it is peaking. The advancement and homogenization of mobile devices has carried with it the ability of every man, woman, and child to do what they want, at the very moment they want. That, in and of itself, creates a giant emerging market that is going to take years to run its course. For now, grab ahold and create your opportunity. Start here today with retail arbitrage. People all over the world are exponentially moving away from brick-and-mortar retail and more and more towards online commerce. The generation entering elementary school today will much prefer internet shopping, and the generation after that will know nothing except internet shopping. We happen to be the generation of people that are familiar equally with both. We are not too early, nor are we too late. We are right in that sweet spot, ready to lay claim to the market as it finds its stride. As you may be thinking, these parting words are not just referring to RA. Rather, I am referring to every endeavor you can learn. I implore you, start your RA business. Get used to it. Streamline it. Then, add something else to your repertoire of web-based ventures. Private labeling, eBooks, affiliate marketing, etc. The possibilities are limited only by your lack of will to continue searching, or your financial comfort level having been met. The possibilities by which to grow your income is a book that has yet to be written. I suggest that you grab a pen and start writing.

50465849R00022

Made in the USA
San Bernardino, CA
23 June 2017